VISTA

AMERICAN SIGN LANGUAGE SERIES

FUNCTIONAL NOTIONAL APPROACH

SIGNING Naturally

STUDENT WORKBOOK

UNITS 7-12

EDITED BY LISA CAHN

DawnSignPress
San Diego, California

W9-AHA-525

Edited by *Lisa Cahn*
Illustrations by *Chuck Baird, Patricia Pearson, Valerie Winemiller*
Sign Illustrations by *Frank Allen Paul, Paul Setzer*

Sign Models

Sandra Ammons   *Ben Bahan*   *Tina Jo Breindel*   *Sue Burnes*

Amanda Cervi   *Bob Hiltermann*   *Anthony Kolombatovic*   *Ken Mikos*   *Erin Paul*

John Reid

Published by DawnSignPress

ISBN: 978-1-58121-215-0

Printed in the United States of America

10   9   8   7   6   5   4

In Hwa Reisig

Quantity discounts and special purchase arrangements for teachers,
schools and bookstores are available. For more information, contact:

DawnSignPress
6130 Nancy Ridge Drive
San Diego, CA 92121-3223
(858) 625-0600 V • (858) 625-2336 Fax
(858) 768-0428 VP
www.dawnsign.com

TABLE OF CONTENTS

INTRODUCTION

Signing Naturally Student Workbook, Units 7-12 is designed to give you a way to review and practice what you learn in the classroom. With video from the DVD, you can see the movement of signs as they are used in a sentence, observe how a sign form is influenced by the sign that precedes or follows, and learn how sign movements can be modified to change meaning. You can see when and how facial expressions occur and how body, head, and eye movements are used for phrasing and agreement. Most important, you see how language is used in context.

Each of the six units revolves around a major language function such as asking for and giving directions, making requests, attributing qualities to others, and talking about routines. Through this functional approach, the language you learn is the language used in everyday conversation. By learning language functions in interactive contexts, you also develop conversational skills in confirming and correcting information, expressing degrees of uncertainty, and asking for clarification and repetition.

There is also a Cumulative Review that focus on specific language and cultural behaviors. You will learn appropriate ways of getting attention, negotiating a signing environment, interrupting conversations, and learn phrases to ask for repetition and to close conversations.

Design of the *DVD* and *Workbook*

The *Student Workbook* is designed to be a guide to the *DVD*. Read the instructions in the workbook before beginning each videotaped activity. Then go back to the workbook for additional activities and readings.

The units are divided into several sections:

1) **LANGUAGE IN ACTION**: Each unit begins with videotaped conversations which are accompanied (in the workbook) by cued dialogues highlighting specific language functions and key phrases. You may see signs or expressions that are unfamiliar. Because of this, we suggest you approach the conversations in the following stages:

   a) Read the situation at the beginning of each cued dialogue in the workbook.
   b) View the conversation and try to follow the intent of the exchange. Do not concern yourself with individual unfamiliar signs.
   c) Read the cued dialogue in the workbook to see if you understood the exchange.
   d) View the conversation again, looking for how key phrases are expressed.
   e) Rehearse the key phrases.

The Conversation Practice section gives you an opportunity to rehearse the key phrases and conversation behaviors with a partner, in situations similar to the ones on screen. To keep it interesting and spontaneous, vary the conversation by adding personal information.

2) **GRAMMAR NOTES:** Grammar features are introduced as needed to express specific language functions. Grammar Notes provide a brief explanation of these features and are usually followed by a videotaped demonstration.

3) **GRAMMAR PRACTICE:** The Grammar Practice videotaped segments focus on language forms and structures in a controlled context. Some of these activities begin with a demonstration of specific grammar features; these are followed by activities that require you to respond to questions, or identify, discriminate, or summarize, and fill in answers in your workbook. Additional Pair Practice activities usually follow, so that you can apply what you learned in conversations with a partner.

4) **COMPREHENSION:** Comprehension activities test your understanding of vocabulary and language functions that you have learned. Narratives are used to help you build your receptive skills, learn vocabulary through context, and develop strategies for figuring out meaning without understanding every sign. These activities also require you to demonstrate your comprehension by filling in your workbook.

5) **CULTURE/LANGUAGE NOTES:** To understand language, you must understand its cultural context. The Culture/Language Notes provide you with a broad overview of the history, values, and social norms of the Deaf community.

6) **VOCABULARY REVIEW:** At the end of each unit in the workbook, you will find sign illustrations of key phrases and vocabulary for that unit. Many of the sign illustrations have a corresponding picture to show the meaning of the sign. Other more abstract vocabulary whose meaning cannot easily be illustrated with pictures are grouped into categories to help you remember the meaning of the sign. We chose not to give you English equivalents because they often restrict your understanding and usage of the signs. All key phrases and vocabulary for each unit is on the DVD.

   Some signs vary from one region to the next. Your instructor may have introduced a different sign more commonly used in your local area than the one used in your workbook. Be sure to remember the local sign, but be aware that there will be different signs used in other parts of the United States and Canada.

An Answer Key is provided at the back so that you can check your answers.

How to Use the *DVD* and *Workbook*

1) Since as much DVD time as possible has been used for language purposes, all instructions for activities are given in the workbook. Remember to read the instructions in the workbook before starting each activity.

2) Most activities on theDVD allow a two- to three-second pause for you to mark your answers. This may not be enough time, so feel free to stop the DVD to give yourself more time to answer.

3) If you miss a sign or sentence while working on an activity, don't rewind to see just that part again, but continue the activity till the end, then replay the whole activity to complete the answers you missed.

4) After you complete a workbook activity, you can video segment for additional language practice. For example, after identifying sentence types, go back and practice signing the sentences.

5) Use the *DVD* as a reference to review and practice what you have learned, to prepare for tests, and to retain your ASL skills during breaks in school sessions.

Strategies for Learning American Sign Language (ASL)

To increase your language learning in the classroom, develop the following habits:

1) Follow all conversations whether they are between the teacher and class, teacher and student, or student and student.

2) Focus on the signer's face, not on the hands. Don't break eye contact while in a signed conversation.

3) Develop active listening behaviors, i.e., nodding, responding with "huh?" "wow," "really?" Your teacher may stop to repeat information because you do not nod to indicate you are following along. This is not teacher/student behavior - it is cultural. Listeners have very active roles in signed conversations.

4) Participate as much as possible by adding comments, agreeing or disagreeing, etc. The more you participate, the more you will retain what you learn. Don't worry about mistakes. They are part of the learning process.

5) Try not to worry about a sign you missed. Work on getting the gist of the conversation. If a particular sign pops up over and over, and you haven't a clue to its meaning, then ask the teacher. Try to avoid asking your classmate for a quick English translation. You would lose out on valuable communication experiences that can strengthen your comprehension skills.

6) Leave English (and your voice) outside the door. Try not to translate in your head as you watch someone sign. Don't worry about memorizing, as repetition and context will help you acquire the language.

7) Try to maintain a signing environment during class breaks, before class begins, and whenever Deaf people are present.

8) Try not to miss class, especially at the beginning. Your class strives to form a language community; the cohesiveness of the group influences how rich the language exchange is in the classroom. Missing class makes it difficult to achieve this interactive environment.

Unit 7
Giving Directions

LANGUAGE IN ACTION

Conversation 1

Kim (A), a Sign Language student, approaches Cinnie (B) in the stairway of a college building to ask directions to the soda machine.

> **A:** explain problem with soda machine, ask if B knows where another soda machine is
> **B: tell where you think one is** (on another floor), ask if A knows where
> **A:** respond negatively
> **B:** check if A knows where the elevator is
> **A:** confirm
> **B: give directions from there**
> **A:** repeat directions to confirm
> **B:** confirm
> **A:** express thanks
> **A and B:** say goodbye

Conversation 2

Ella (B) and Ken (C) are sitting outdoors, chatting over lunch. Ben (A) joins them and asks Ella where he can buy a sandwich.

> **A, B and C:** greet each other
> **A:** (to B) say that you're hungry, explain you forgot to bring a sandwich, ask where B got her sandwich
> **B:** explain that you brought it from home
> **A:** respond, **ask where you can buy** one
> **B: point to location**
> **A:** ask if it's near the bookstore
> **B:** correct, **give more specific location**, check with C to confirm
> **C:** (to A) **give more specific information**
> **A:** respond, ask if you can leave your jacket, give reason; **say that you will be back**
> **B and C:** agree
> **A:** express thanks (leave)
> **B and C:** (continue conversation)

Key phrases that express target language functions are highlighted. Replay the videotape until you can follow the conversations without the aid of the cues. Then rehearse both conversations, especially the key phrases.

CONVERSATION PRACTICE

To practice the key phrases in a new context, find a partner and role play the following situations:

1

Situation 1: A new student in class asks you how to get to the nearest bus stop. (Other possible locations: gym, park, grocery store, swimming pool, etc.)

Situation 2: Approach an information desk in a large office complex and ask where a certain room or office is located.

GRAMMAR NOTES

Cardinal and Ordinal Numbers

By now you have learned the basic handshapes for cardinal (or counting) numbers. While the handshapes remain the same, different movements and locations are used for different kinds of numbers, i.e., age numbers, ordinal numbers, money numbers. In this unit, we focus on ordinal numbers.

Ordinal numbers indicate order in a series. These numbers have the following forms:

"first" to "ninth"   Made with a twist of the wrist towards the body, with the hand in a more horizontal position than the position for cardinal numbers.

"tenth" and up   Usually made with the same form as cardinal numbers, but adding fingerspelled "th" at the end. Sometimes just the number is used if the context is clear.

Ordinal Numbers

On screen, Ken will model ordinal numbers "first" to "tenth." Replay the tape and practice signing the numbers.

GRAMMAR NOTES

Giving Directions

To give directions to a place in a building, go from general to specific. For example, to give directions to the teacher's office:

1) Give the general location: "upstairs, on the fourth floor"
2) Identify a starting point on that floor: "as you leave the elevator. . ."
3) Give specific directions from the starting point: "turn left, pass the drinking fountain, and it's the second door on your right"

To give directions to someone familiar with the building, use a **common reference point** (i.e., that you and the listener both know). For example, for the same teacher's office:

1) Establish a common reference point: "you know the drinking fountain on the fourth floor?"
2) Give specific directions to the desired location: "pass the drinking fountain, and it's the second door on the right"

Use the skills described in "Spatial Agreement" in Unit 3, i.e., eye gaze/location agreement and non-manual behaviors showing relative distance, so that your listener can visualize the route or location you describe.

Mary will model giving directions in the next videotaped activity.

GRAMMAR PRACTICE

Giving Directions

Ben will ask Mary where he can find various things in the building illustrated below. Find #1 on the illustration, then watch Mary give directions to that location. Then do the same for #2 and #3.

Giving Directions Using a Common Reference

Again, Ben will ask Mary where he can find various things in the building. Watch how she signs directions to locations marked #4, #5 and #6 in the illustration. Notice how she establishes a common reference point.

Rewind the tape to the beginning of this activity. After Ben signs each question, stop the tape and give directions. Then compare your directions with Mary's.

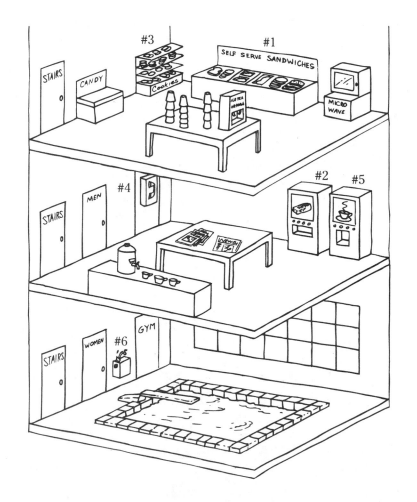

PAIR PRACTICE

Practice 1. Find a partner and go to a building with several floors. Divide the floors up between yourselves; for example, you go to the first and second floors while your partner goes to the third and fourth floors. Take a short tour of your floors to familiarize yourself with the locations of various places. Then give your partner a list of places on those floors that s/he could ask about.

Ask each other where the things or places on your lists are located. Practice giving directions, going from general to specific as described in the Grammar Note above.

Practice 2. Go to a location that you and your partner are familiar with. Collect several things, such as a book, jacket, candy bar, and put them in other rooms. Your partner is to ask where each thing is located. Establish a common reference point as you give directions to the location of each object.

COMPREHENSION

Fingerspelling, Part 3

Five signers will sign a total of 12 sentences with one fingerspelled word in each. You are to write down the word that is spelled. You don't need to write the whole sentence.

1. _ice_
2. _TV_   _twice_
3. _diet_
4. _Coke_
5. _oil_
6. _fan_   _up - down_

7. _HS_
8. _apt_   _just down_
9. _7-UP_   _7-thumbs up_
10. _TTY_
11. _Von_
12. _Cake_

Answers on page 101.

PAIR PRACTICE

Sign sentences to your partner, using one fingerspelled word in each sentence (fingerspell words and abbreviated forms from both your list above and the list below). Have your partner repeat the fingerspelled word you used.

bus	car	dept (department)	ID (identification)
toy	bag	ref (refrigerator)	gas
OK	job	OT (overtime)	VCR

The Candy Bar

Ben tells a story about a person waiting in an airport lounge for a delayed flight. Write a summary of the story.

Summary given on page 101.

CULTURE/LANGUAGE NOTES

Cross-Cultural Communication

Ninety percent of all deaf children have hearing parents. A small percentage of these parents learn Sign Language. Consequently, Deaf people at a very early age develop strategies for communicating with people who do not sign. Some of the the most common strategies are described below:

Pen and paper are used for seeking information, conducting business (i.e., getting directions, placing orders), or having conversations. This is the most common strategy for cross-cultural communication.

Gesturing is usually used with people seen regularly and in situations where the interaction is predictable. This form of communication is used to manage limited social contact with people like the regular waitress at the local coffee shop, relatives, co-workers, neighbors. If the interaction continues, other strategies such as pen and paper are usually used.

Lipreading and speech are among the least preferred strategies for most Deaf people. Approximately thirty percent of spoken English can be understood by lipreading, which leaves the Deaf person in an untenable position. This percentage can increase if the hearing person or the subject is familiar, or if the content is predictable (i.e., "how are you?" in a greeting). Lipreading leaves considerable room for misunderstanding, and because of this, it is held to a minimum. The use of speech varies with each individual. Few Deaf people feel comfortable using speech with strangers.

Adapting signs to others (or modifying Sign Language for communicative purposes) is used with hearing people with varying degrees of signing ability. Deaf people will vary their signs to match the language skills of the other person. This might mean the inclusion of more fingerspelled words, more mouthing of words, gesturing, simple sentences, slower pace, more English-like word order. The goal is to communicate, so Deaf people will use whatever combination of methods is most effective. This is similar to what you would do with a person who is obviously foreign born and not fluent in the English language.

Using a third person to interpret is another strategy to help make conversations between Deaf and hearing persons flow more smoothly. The third person would sign what was said and voice what was signed. In many situations such as medical, legal, educational and professional, Deaf people prefer to use certified Sign Language interpreters who not only know the language fluently, but are sensitive to Deaf and hearing cultures as well.

Strategies for Sign Language students:
- Let the Deaf person know that you can sign.
- Let the Deaf person set the communication pattern to be used.
- Avoid talking (using voice) in the presence of a Deaf person without relaying the information in signs. It is considered rude not to keep the Deaf person informed.
- If you see other people signing, avoid watching their conversation unless you intend to introduce yourself.

End of Unit 7

5

KEY PHRASES

Explain need (hungry), ask where restaurant is

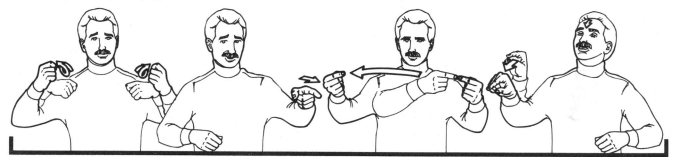

Tell where (across from the gym)

Explain problem (locked bathroom), ask where's another

VOCABULARY REVIEW

PLACES

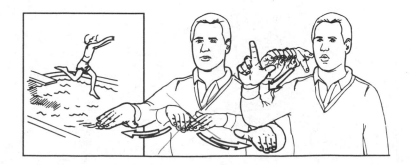

**WITHIN THE
BUILDING**

basement

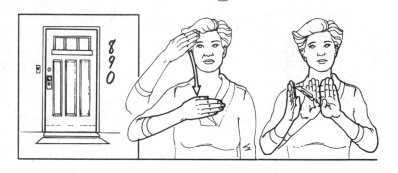

INDICATING LOCATIONS

enter

out

need to

across

PROBLEMS

broken

not

washing

?

closed?

locked

dirty

warm

SNACKS

COOKIE

CHOCO

gum

vs. ole computer

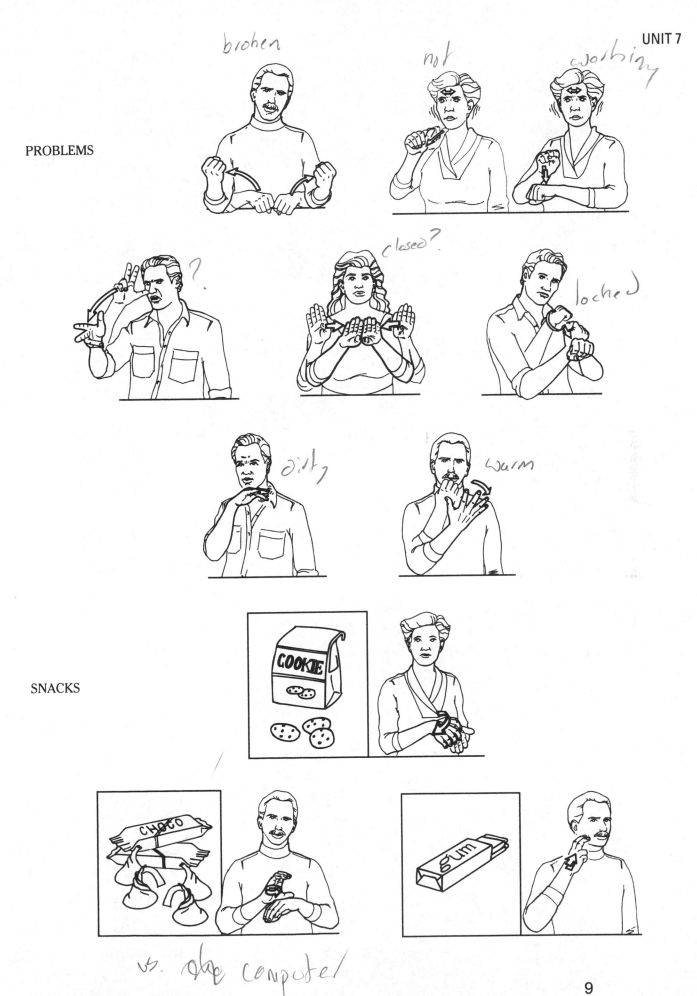

spell

vs. Italian

sandwhich

eat
sandwhich

suction

cig

sugar

vs. cute

EXPRESS NEEDS

thirsty

hunger

need

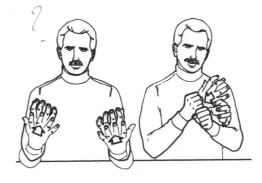

most

searching

SIZES OF DRINKS

some
medium

large

WITH/WITHOUT

with

without

11

EXPRESSING DEGREES OF CERTAINTY

Certain   Somewhat   Uncertain
uncertain

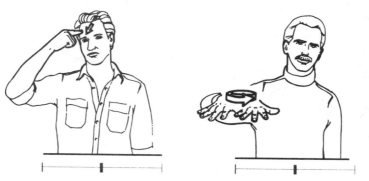

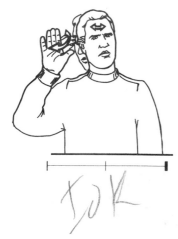

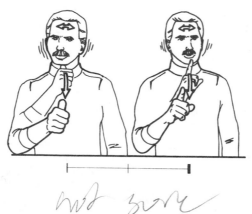

Unit 8
Describing Others

LANGUAGE IN ACTION

Conversation 1

Flo (A) is walking her dog in a park when she runs into Mary (B).

   A: (walking dog)
   B: greet B with surprise
   A: greet A with surprise, ask if she lives here
   B: reply affirmatively, explain that you brought kids here to play
   A: express surprise, ask if B has children
   B: explain they're your husband's children from his first marriage
   A: ask where the kids are on the playground
   B: identify daughter
   A: give additional descriptions to confirm
   B: confirm
   B: identify son
   A: give additional descriptions to confirm
   B: confirm
   A: make comment, ask if kids are deaf
   B: tell that one is deaf, and one is hearing
   A: explain that you live nearby, that you could come back (dog pulls leash) and that the dog
      wants to go
   A and B: say goodbye

Conversation 2

Brian (A), the father of a young boy, approaches the person (B) working at the lost and found office at a public pool.

   A and B: greet each other
   A: explain that your son lost two pieces of clothing, request help
   B: ask for description
   A: describe items
   B: repeat descriptions to make sure
   A: confirm
   B: tell that you'll go look for them (leave and return with items), ask if first item is correct
   A: (check jacket), **confirm**
   B: (hand over second item)
   A: (check shorts) **correct description** for shorts
   B: repeat correct description (go look again and return), **express regret**
   A: complain about son losing things, express thanks
   B: say goodbye

Key phrases that express target language functions are highlighted. Replay the videotape until you can follow the conversations without the aid of the cues. Then rehearse both conversations, especially the key phrases.

CONVERSATION PRACTICE

To practice the key phrases in a new context, find a partner and role play the situations below:

Situation 1: You are at a convention. You need to get a message to a person waiting in the lobby that you will be delayed 30 minutes. Your friend is willing to relay the message but doesn't know what the person looks like. (Possible person: your sister, your spouse, your parent, your daughter or son, your aunt or uncle, your girlfriend or boyfriend.)

Situation 2: People at your office are pooling money to buy a gift for a co-worker. You're in charge of buying the gift. Unsure of the person's taste in clothes, you consult others.

GRAMMAR NOTES

Identifying Others

There are certain norms to follow for identifying and describing people:

- Point out the person and describe his/her most noticeable or distinguishing characteristics (see list below for what to describe).
- Make sure your listener understands who you're talking about - do not go on until you get **confirmation** that s/he knows who you mean. Identifying people is an **interactive** process.

The way you identify someone varies slightly depending on whether the person is present and within sight or not present.

If you want to identify someone who is **present and within sight**, begin your sentence with raised eyebrows and this sign:

Then point to the person and describe him/her, keeping your eyebrows raised throughout the description. Descriptions of people tend to follow a particular order. Gender is always mentioned first; then, in general:

- height
- body type
- color of hair
- hairstyle

Other characteristics are mentioned right after gender if they distinguish the person from others in that situation (i.e., race, distinctive facial features, eyeglasses, jewelry, clothing, and whether s/he is sitting, standing, or signing).

When your listener nods or gives confirming descriptions of the person you identified, proceed with comments or questions about that person.

If you want to identify someone who is **not present**, begin your sentence with raised eyebrows and this sign:

Then go on to describe the person in the same general order, adding information about where the listener might have seen the person. If the listener indicates that s/he doesn't know who you mean, continue your description with occupation, personal qualities, habits, and the person's relationship to other people the listener knows. When the listener indicates (with a nod or confirming question) that s/he recognizes the person you identified, continue with your comments or question.

In the next activity, Ben will model how to identify people present in the room, and Mary will model how to confirm or acknowledge that she knows who he means.

GRAMMAR PRACTICE

Identifying Others

On screen Ben and Mary will first demonstrate how to identify and acknowledge others in the room. This is followed by four dialogues showing different ways of identifying people. Pay particular attention to how the listener confirms which person the speaker is referring to; notice that the speaker does not proceed until the listener confirms the right person.

Dialogue 1

Ben: **identify** person (by gender, color and style of hair, facial feature)

Mary: **confirm** (by adding information about clothing)

Ben: **confirm** that it's the right person, then ask question

Mary: give information

Ben: respond

Dialogue 2

Mary: **identify** person (by gender and distinctive facial feature)

Ben: **confirm** (by adding information about body type)

Mary: **confirm** that it's the right person, give information

Ben: respond

Dialogue 3

Mary: **identify** person (by gender, height, and hairstyle)

Ben: **confirm** (by adding information about body type)

Mary: **correct** (by adding information about location of person

Ben: **acknowledge**, **confirm** (by adding description of clothing)

Mary: **confirm**, give information

Ben: respond

Dialogue 4

Ben: **identify** person (by gender, eyeglasses, location)

Mary: **confirm** (by describing hairstyle)

Ben: **correct** (by emphasizing eyeglasses)

Mary: **acknowledge**

Ben: ask information

Mary: give information

Ben: comment

Mary: agree

PAIR PRACTICE

Find a partner and practice identifying others who are present and within sight. Follow the cued dialogues above to practice different ways of identifying people and different sequences of acknowledging the person. (Possible environments: lobby of a hotel, beach, railroad station, coffee shop.)

Numbers: Multiples of 10 and 11

Cinnie will model numbers in multiples of 10 (from 20 to 100), and then Brian will model numbers in multiples of 11 (from 11 to 99). Replay the tape and practice signing the numbers.

COMPREHENSION

Personal Data

Ben will give you personal information about each of the people pictured below. Write the information he gives under the appropriate picture. Stop the tape after each sentence to give yourself time to write.

is deaf

was married now divorced

name is Jamie

go to movies

name is sean

has 6 children

Answers on page 101.

PAIR PRACTICE

Give additional information to your partner about each person pictured above. First identify the person, then wait until your partner acknowledges the right person before you give the information. Each of you should write down the information given.

Missing Number

Different signers will give you sequences of numbers (multiples of 5, 10 and 11). Figure out the number missing from each sequence. Write down only the number that's missing.

Example: _____20_____   3. _____

  1. _____   4. _____

  2. _____   5. _____

Answers given on page 101.

End of Unit 8

KEY PHRASES

Identify person

Ask for confirmation

Confirm, ask who

Describe clothing

19

Correct description

Describe change in appearance

VOCABULARY REVIEW

ETHNICITY

DESCRIBE HAIR

Hair lengths

Hair types

**DESCRIBE
FACES**

Shape of faces

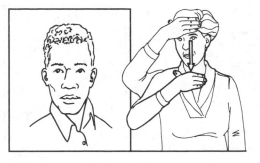

Facial hair

Facial features

DESCRIBE HEIGHTS

DESCRIBE
BODY TYPES

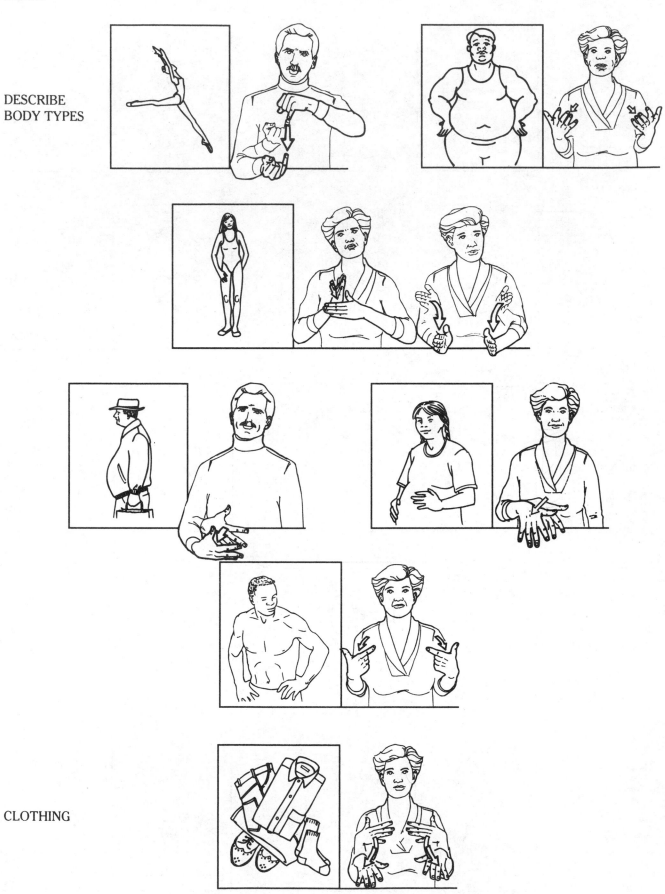

CLOTHING

25

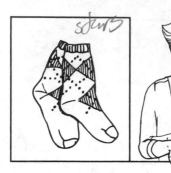

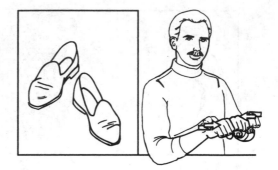

STYLES OF CLOTHING

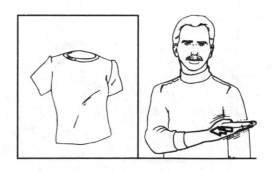

PATTERNS
ON CLOTHES

ACCESSORIES

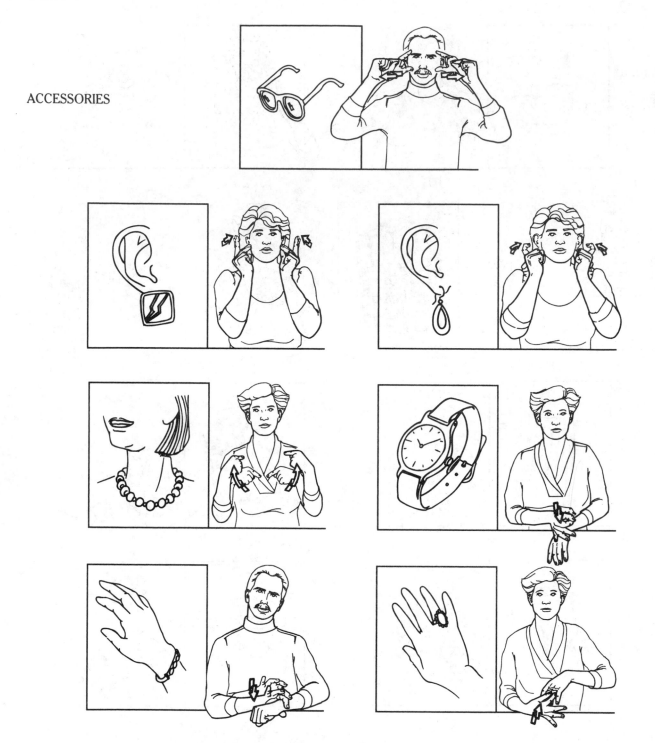

NUMBERS

Multiples of 10 and 11

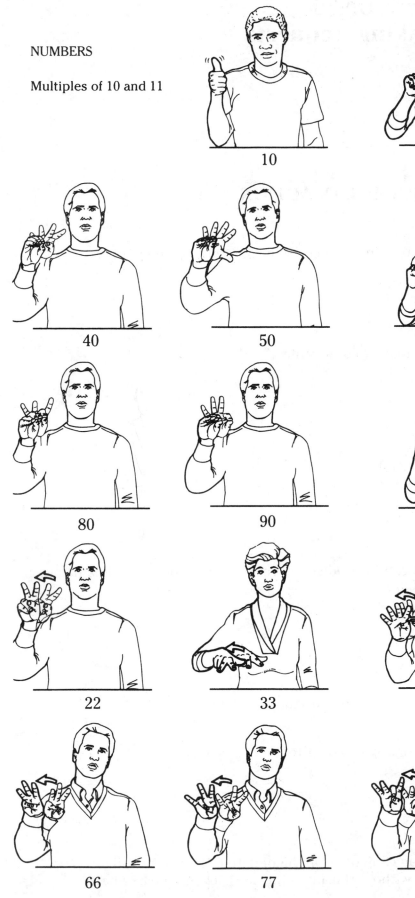

10

20

30

40

50

60

70

80

90

100

11

22

33

44

55

66

77

88

99

29

Unit 9
Making Requests

LANGUAGE IN ACTION

Conversation 1

Two friends are getting ready for a party. Ben (A) is cooking something in the kitchen when Ken (B) arrives with a bag of groceries.

B: make comment
A: request help
B: agree, ask what you can do
A: request that he bring over a neighbor's folding table
B: accept, ask where it is
A: tell where to go get it
B: identify neighbor to confirm
A: confirm
B: respond, ask where to put it
A: tell where
B: respond, tell that you are going to get it now
A: (remember something), ask another favor
B: respond, offer more help
A: express thanks

Conversation 2

Cinnie (A) is visiting Ella (B). Cinnie is getting ready to leave. She remembers that Ella has to submit a report for class, so she asks her about it.

A: ask if B has completed the report
B: reply negatively, explain why
A: offer assistance (babysitting)
B: accept offer
A: ask when a good time would be
B: explain that the report is due Monday, suggest the Saturday before
A: agree
B: express thanks
A: accept, leavetaking (stand up and nearly trip over toy)
B: apologize
A: offer to help clean up
B: decline, tell why
A: agree
A and B: say goodbye

Key phrases that express target language functions are highlighted. Replay the videotape until you can follow the conversations without the aid of the cues. Then rehearse both conversations, especially the key phrases.

30

CONVERSATION PRACTICE

To practice the key phrases in a new context, find a partner and role play the situations below:

Situation 1: Your partner is complaining about something. Offer assistance. (Possible complaints: house is a mess, TV is on the blink, faucet is leaking, need a hair cut, grass in yard is overgrown, basketball hoop fell down, etc.)

Situation 2: Your friend plans to go to the store and asks you if there's anything you need. Possible needs:

- milk (specify size)
- toothpaste (specify tube or pump)
- dog food (specify brand and size)
- laundry detergent (specify size and describe the box)

GRAMMAR NOTES

Money Numbers

Money numbers, like ordinal numbers described in Unit 7, have their own distinctive forms. In this unit we focus on the numbers expressing how many cents.

The form for money numbers under a dollar is a combination of the sign "cent" (index finger moving out from the forehead) and the number. Some signers may fingerspell "cents" after the number is signed, i.e., 77 cents, 39 cents.

The form for "1 dollar" is similar to the ordinal number "first." "1 dollar" can be made with a slightly bigger twist of the wrist and with a wider arc than the ordinal number. You may have to rely on context to distinguish whether it's "first" or "1 dollar" that's being signed.

You will see examples of money numbers in the next videotaped segment.

GRAMMAR PRACTICE

Money Numbers

Mary will model money numbers for 1, 5, 10, 15, 20, and 25 cents. She will then model money numbers in tens from 60 to 90 cents, and in tens from 55 to 95 cents. Finally, she will model the sign for 1 dollar.

Notice where her palm faces for each number sign. Replay the tape and imitate each sign.

GRAMMAR NOTES

Verb Types

There are three types of verbs in ASL: plain, inflecting, and spatial.*

Plain verbs require the signer to specify the subject and object. Consider the verbs below. If you use them in a sentence, you have to explicitly mention who is doing what with whom; the verbs themselves do not convey that information.

Inflecting verbs, unlike plain verbs, allow the signer to indicate the subject and object by changing the direction of movement of the sign. Consider the first two signs below: the signs start at the subject and end at the object. The verb can also be inflected to indicate the number of subjects and/or objects - see the third illustration below.

| (I to you) | (s/he to me) | (I to all of you) |

Spatial verbs, like inflecting verbs, allow the signer to change the direction of movement of the sign to indicate location (i.e., from here to there). Like plain verbs, however, the subject and object must be specified. For example:

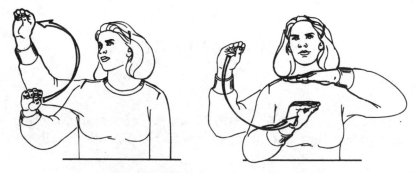

*This breakdown of verb types is from Carol Padden, "Interaction of Morphology and Syntax in American Sign Language " unpublished doctoral dissertation, 1983, University of California, San Diego.

GRAMMAR PRACTICE

Verb Types: Skit 1, 2, 3

On screen you will observe three different skits. Each skit will be followed by a narrator summarizing what happened. In each narrative, observe how spatial and inflecting verbs are used. Mary narrates Skit 1 using spatial verbs; Cinnie and Ben narrate Skits 2 and 3 using inflecting verbs.

After you have seen all the skits and narratives, replay each skit and narrate what happened. Compare your narrative with the one that follows on screen.

COMPREHENSION

Give and Take

Ella will sign five accounts of three people giving and taking money. She will ask a question at the end of each account about how much money one person has. Stop the tape and write your answers below.

	Who?	*How Much?*
1.	Sally	none
2.	Jane	35 cents
3.	Bob	none
4.	Bob	30 cents
5.	Sally	30 cents

Answers on page 102.

Making Requests

On screen five signers will sign narratives about making requests. Write the letter that appears on screen next to the picture that matches the narrative. If you need more time, stop the tape after each narrative.

A

33

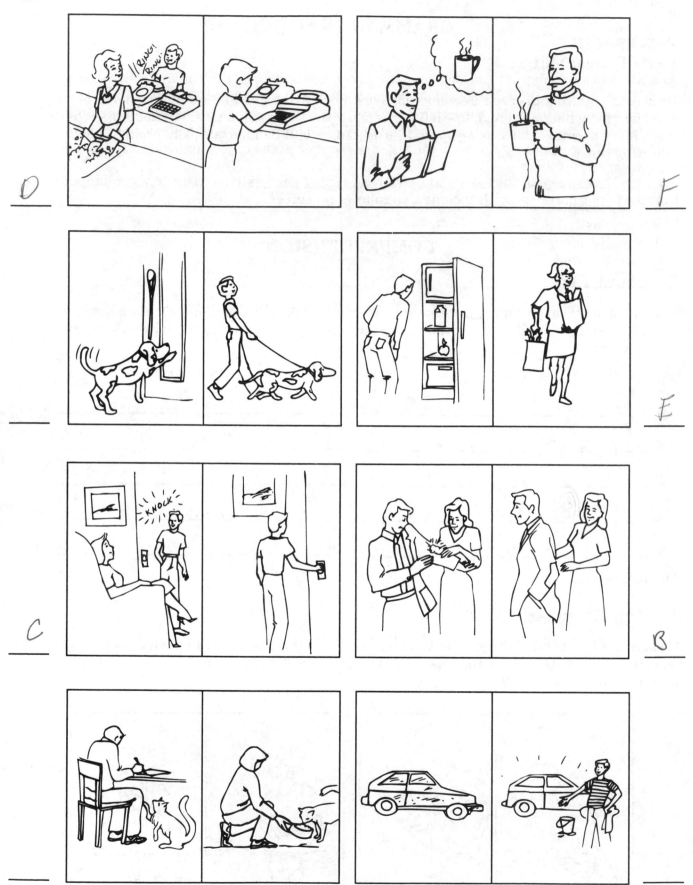

Answers on page 102,103

34

PAIR PRACTICE

Practice making requests by asking your partner to get the objects pictured on the following page. First, decide which of you will assign locations for the numbered objects, and which of you will assign locations for the lettered objects. Write the numbers (or letters) of the objects in different locations in the kitchen pictured below. When done, follow the dialogue format below, and have your partner mark the letter or number of the object in the location specified. Take turns being Signer A.

A: give reason, request that B get an object from the kitchen
B: agree, ask where
A: identify location, tell where object is in relation to that location
B: (mark corresponding location in your picture)

Afterwards, compare pictures to check that you each marked the correct location for each object.

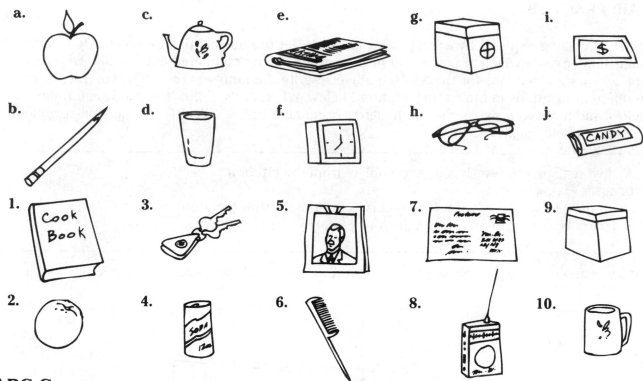

ABC Gum

Ella tells a story about a boy who is not supposed to have gum. One day while he's chewing gum his mother calls him. He sticks the gum on the bench, then goes off. The story goes on to tell what happened to the gum.

Write a summary of the story. Include the different places the gum ended up, and how each person found it.

Summary given on page 103.

End of Unit 9

KEY PHRASES

Make request (to close window)

Make request (to borrow a dollar)

Agree to request   Agree to request   Agree to request for help

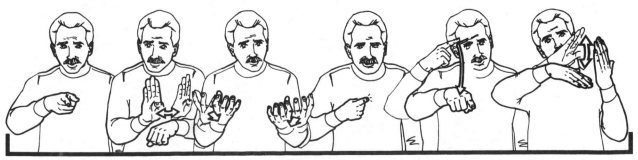

Offer assistance (to paint)

37

Offer assistance (to assemble)

Accept assistance

Accept assistance

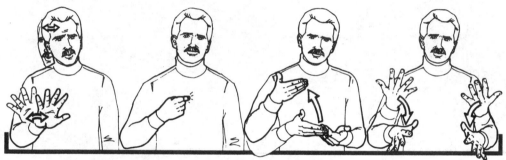

Decline assistance (almost done)

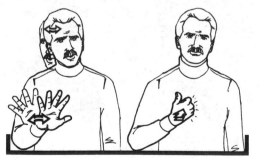

Decline assistance (will do it yourself)

VOCABULARY REVIEW

INFLECTING VERBS

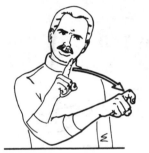 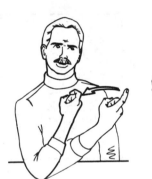  

SPATIAL VERBS

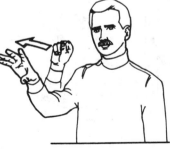

**OBJECTS AROUND
THE ROOM**

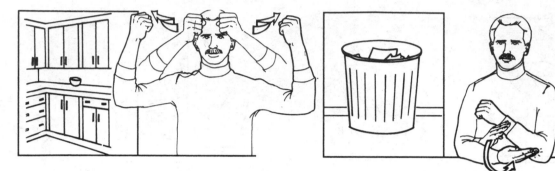

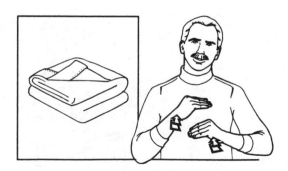

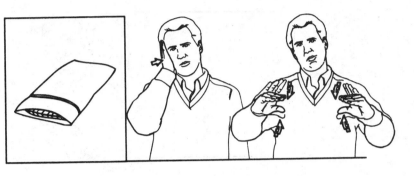

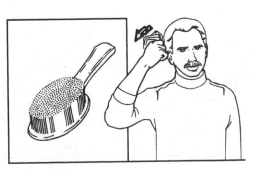

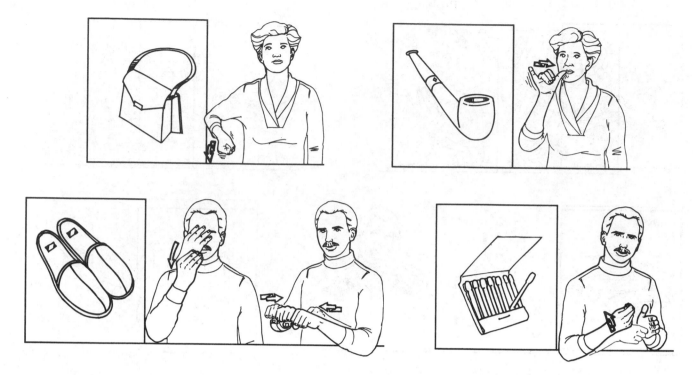

PROBLEMS
AND
REQUESTS

Problem

Request

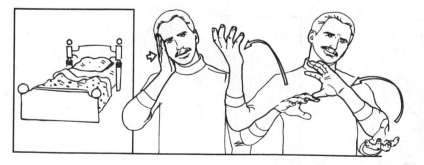

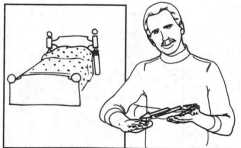

Problem | Request

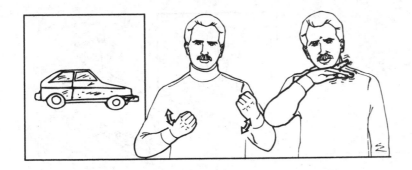 

 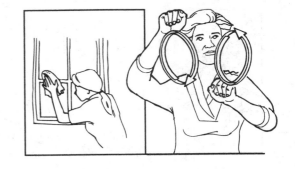

 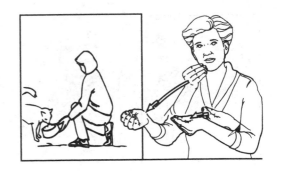

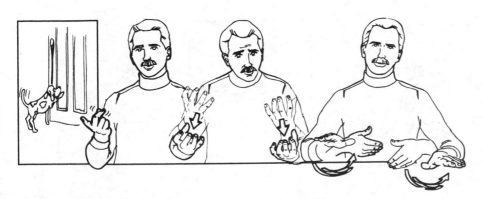 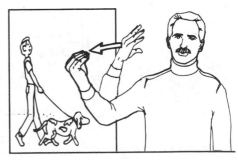

Problem   Request

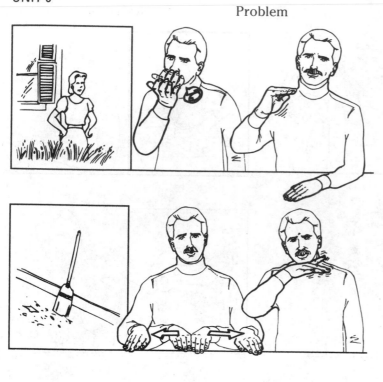

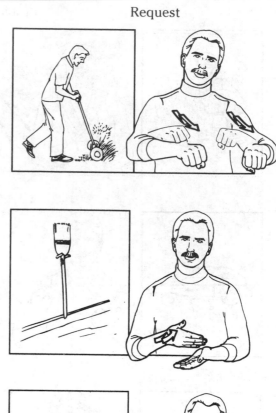

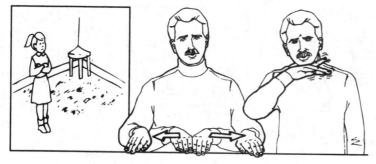

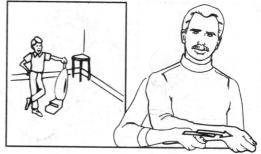

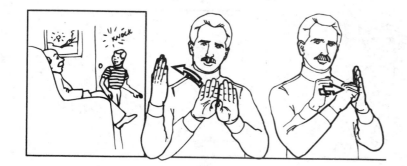

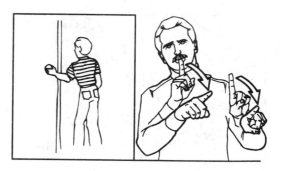

Problem

Request

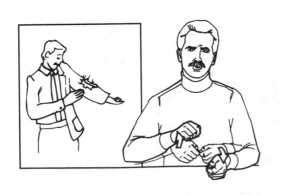

45

Problem   Request

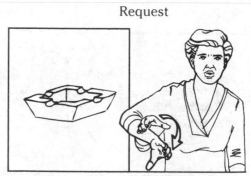

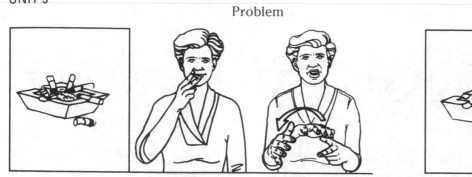

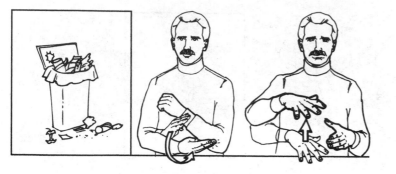

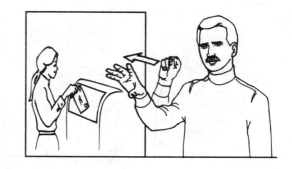

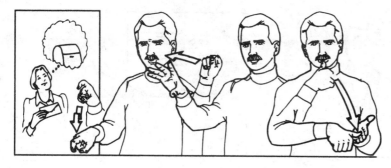

STAGES OF
COMPLETION

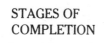

not   completed
started

MONEY NUMBERS

1¢

5¢

10¢

15¢

20¢

25¢

50¢

55¢

60¢

65¢

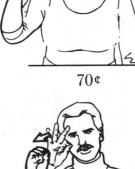
70¢

75¢

80¢

85¢

90¢

95¢

$1.00

Unit 10
Talking About Family and Occupations

LANGUAGE IN ACTION

Conversation 1

Brian (B) missed work last Friday. On Monday, Mary (A) asks Brian about his absence.

A: greet B, ask about absence
B: give explanation (parents' wedding anniversary)
A: **ask how long** parents have been married
B: **tell how long**
A: respond, ask how many brothers and sisters B has
B: tell how many, **tell where you rank among siblings**
A: ask where siblings live
B: **tell where each one lives**
A: comment, **ask if siblings are close to each other**
B: **reply**
A: respond

Conversation 2

Flo (A), an employer, is interviewing Ben (B), a job applicant.

A: **ask if B is working** right now
B: reply affirmatively and **tell where**
A: **ask about tasks performed**
B: **explain tasks**
A: ask if B likes his present job
B: reply affirmatively
A: **ask if B gets along with others at work**
B: reply affirmatively

Key phrases that express target language functions are highlighted. Replay the videotape until you can follow the conversations without the aid of the cues. Then rehearse both conversations, especially the key phrases.

CONVERSATION PRACTICE

To practice the key phrases in a new context, find a partner and role play the situations below:

Situation 1: You are at the 20-year reunion of your high school class. You would like to tell a former classmate about what you've been doing all these years. Tell about your spouse/relationship and children. Tell how long you've been in the relationship and how old each child is.

Situation 2: You are interviewing people to find participants for Career Day at a local high school. Ask your partner to explain his/her job.

GRAMMAR NOTES

Personal and Possessive Pronouns

Personal pronouns (I, you, s/he) are signed with the index finger. Possessive pronouns (my, your, his/her) are signed with the B-handshape (with thumb extended).

Pronouns	English	ASL
personal:	I/me	index finger points to yourself
	you	index finger points to the person you are talking to
	he/she/it him/her	index finger points to the person (if present) or to space designating that person*
possessive:	my/mine	pat your chest with B-hand
	your/yours	B-hand faces the person(s) you are talking to
	his/her/its	B-hand faces the third person (if present) or to space designating that person*

Age Numbers

Forming Age Numbers. The sign form for **age numbers** is a combination of the sign indicating age and the number itself. To indicate age, the index finger contacts the chin (the contraction of the sign for "old") and is followed by the number. There is a variation where the sign for "old" in its original form is used in conjunction with the number. On videotape you will see the contracted form for showing age numbers. Pay attention to which direction Cinnie's palm is facing as she signs the numbers.

Ranking by Age. When talking about three or more children or siblings in a family, you would usually **rank each child by age** on your non-dominant hand. The oldest is represented by the thumb or index finger, depending on the number. You can continue to give additional information by simply pointing to the finger representing that family member.

Observe how this is done in the "Talking About Children" segment on screen.

*If you are talking about a person who is not present in the room, first indicate who and designate a space to your right or left to represent that person. Then every time you point to that designated space, it functions like "he" or "she." You should continue using the same point of reference as long as you are talking about that person.

GRAMMAR PRACTICE

Age Numbers

Cinnie will model age numbers for 1 to 20 years old. Replay the tape and practice signing the numbers.

Talking About Children

You will see four signers talk about their children. Observe when and how the signers use ranking to talk about children.

Signer #1: has one child
Signer #2: has two children   (contrastive structure used)
Signer #3: has three children   (ranking used)
Signer #4: has six children   (ranking used)

Notice how the signer talks about the sixth child in the family. He signs the ordinal number sixth with his non-dominant hand and points to it with his other hand.

Watch Signer #4 again and write down the information given about each of the six children.

#1 _male, 36, married, works as a printer_
#2 _male, 33, divorced, teaches at a state school for the deaf_
#3 _female 31, married, works w/ computers_
#4 _female 28, not married, works at bank_
#5 _male 28, married separated, searching for job_
#6 _female 24 at University, dating a boy_

Answers on page 103.

COMPREHENSION

A Show of Hands

Two contestants appear on the game show, "A Show of Hands: Deaf Trivia." The host of the show begins by interviewing each contestant.

Watch the whole segment, then go back and watch it again to answer the following questions:

1. What personal information did each contestant give?

Contestant 1: _Carla, my family lives far not here today, not married_
2 brothers, shes the oldest, manages a factory.

Contestant 2: _Janie, married w/ 4 children. girl 7, girl 6, boy 4, boy 3, works at hospital in the lab._

2. What was the first question asked?

name 3 deaf printers

3. What answers did Carol (Cinnie) give?

NAD, dawn sign press,

4. What was the second question asked?

name 3 deaf female artist

5. What answers did Janie (Mary) give?

Betty Miller, Regina o hughes, Linda Bove

6. Which answer was incorrect and why?

Linda Bove is an actress not artist

7. What correct answer did Carol (Cinnie) give instead?

Linda Tom

Answers on page 103, 104.

Fingerspelling, Part 4

In each segment you will see three fingerspelled words. All three words have a common two- or three-letter combination. Write down the common letter combination from the list below. The activity begins with an example.

OY	PH	CH	GL	WI	NN
BR	NT	TT	GHT	ING	EE

Example __CH__

1. _WIWF_   5. _NN_

2. _EE_   6. _ING_

3. _NT_   7. _GL_

4. _OY_   8. _GHT_

Answer on page 104.

End of Unit 10

KEY PHRASES

Ask how old person is

Ask how old when person first flew

Ask how old person started to read

Tell when you did it (34 years old)

Tell you have never done it

Ask where person ranks among children

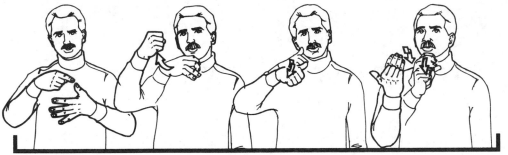

Tell age of oldest child (15 years old)

Ask how long the two of them have been married

Ask how long person worked for a company

Tell how long (7 years)

Tell how long (4 months)

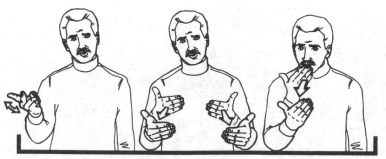

Ask if the two of them get along

VOCABULARY REVIEW

WORKPLACES

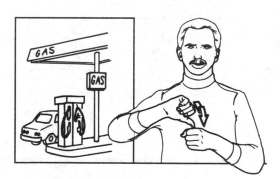

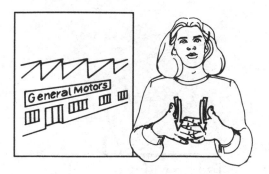

HOSPITAL RELATED
ACTIVITIES

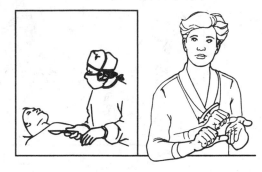

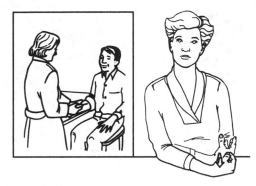

OCCUPATIONS

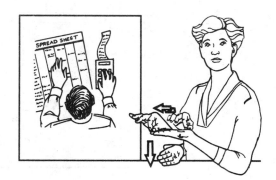

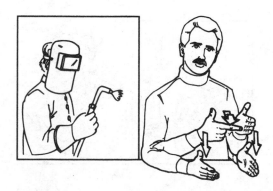

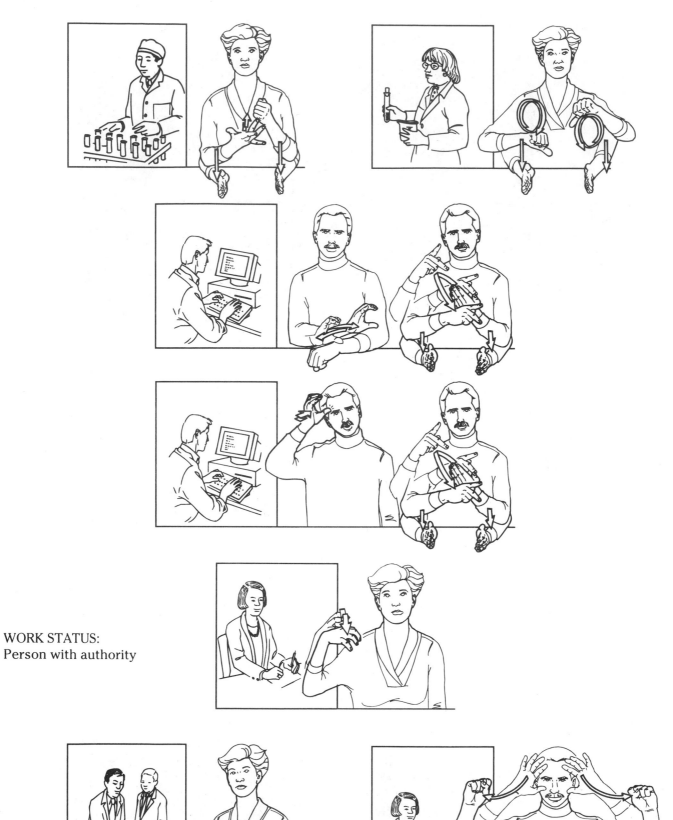

WORK STATUS:
Person with authority

EMPLOYMENT STATUS

TELL HOW PEOPLE
GET ALONG

TELL HOW PEOPLE
DO NOT GET ALONG

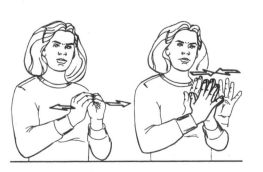

PRONOUNS

"two of us"  "two of them"

"any of them"  "all of them"

"they"

AGE NUMBERS

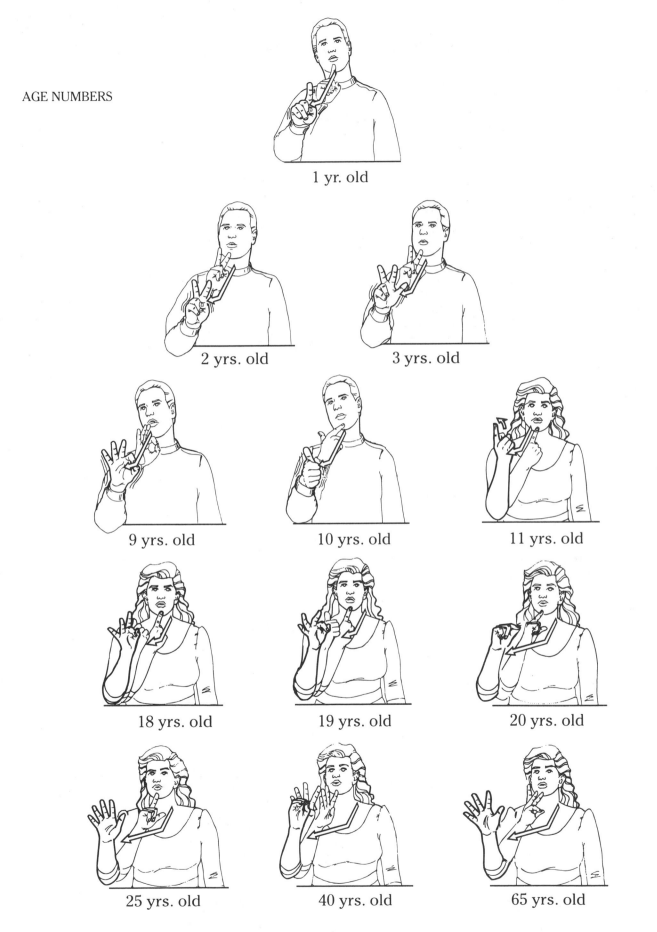

1 yr. old

2 yrs. old

3 yrs. old

9 yrs. old

10 yrs. old

11 yrs. old

18 yrs. old

19 yrs. old

20 yrs. old

25 yrs. old

40 yrs. old

65 yrs. old

Unit 11
Attributing Qualities to Others

LANGUAGE IN ACTION

Conversation 1

Ken (A) asks Mary (B) about a professor that he will have next semester.

A: tell B that you plan to take a class with a certain professor, ask if B has had that professor before
B: respond affirmatively
A: ask B's opinion of the professor
B: give opinion, **describe him (appearance, personality and behavior traits)**
A: respond; ask if you would like the teacher
B: assure A, but tell what A must do to pass the course
A: respond

Conversation 2

Ella (B) is studying in a student lounge. Cinnie (A) enters. She has just met a famous movie star.

A and B: greet each other
A: express excitement, tell news, check if B knows who you mean
B: affirm
A: give your impression of her personality
B: disagree, tell what you read about her
A: express doubt, ask which newspaper
B: give name of newspaper
A: give opinion of newspaper, **correct popular opinion of the person**
B: respond

Key phrases that express target language functions are highlighted. Replay the videotape until you can follow the conversations without the aid of the cues. Then rehearse both conversations, especially the key phrases.

CONVERSATION PRACTICE

To practice the key phrases in a new context, find a partner and role play the situations below:

Situation 1: You and a friend are reminiscing about memorable teachers you've had. Talk about three teachers and include the following about each one:

- physical descriptions
- positive and negative attributes
- any peculiarities in manner

Situation 2: You just read an article about a notable person that suggests s/he isn't what s/he appears to be. Summarize the article to your partner.

GRAMMAR NOTES

Numbers: 67-98

Some of the numbers 67 - 98 are unique in their forms because of the twisting movement of the wrist. For the first set of numbers, 67, 68, 69, 78, 79, 89, the wrist twists one way. For the second set of numbers, 76, 86, 87, 97, 98, the wrist twists the other way.

On screen, Brian will model both sets of numbers. Pay attention to the wrist movement, and where the number begins and where it ends. Go back and review this section frequently to practice reading these numbers; they are the hardest numbers to read.

Role Shifting

Role shifting occurs when a signer describes a person or character, tells what a person did or said, or shows how a person thinks or feels. This is done by "assuming the role" of that person and adopting his/her manner while recounting what was said or done.

In the classroom you have been introduced to one form of role shifting. You learned to adopt the manner and facial expressions associated with specific attributes, such as shyness, anger, humility, boldness.

There are more complex ways of using role shifting where whole conversations are represented. Role shifting makes the recounting of interaction clearer and more interesting. Role shifting is not just a style; it is the "way of telling" preferred in the Deaf community.

You will see examples of role shifting on screen in the three signed narratives that follow. Notice especially how the signer's eye gaze and head position shift, s/he assumes a role. (To see more examples of role shifting, replay any of the videotaped narratives.)

GRAMMAR PRACTICE

Describing Characters

Ben, Cinnie, and Mary will describe major characters from three classic films, *The Ten Commandments*, *The Sound of Music* and *Gone With the Wind*. Observe how they use role shifting when describing each character.

After each narrative, stop the tape and write down the name of each character described, then write the characteristic that best describes each one.

The Ten Commandments

Characters	Characteristics
priest?, pharoh	mean ego, rich
Jewish slaves	fear, anxious, complain
moses	good, humble, wise, irony

The Sound of Music

Characters	Characteristics
Baron Von Trapp	good looking, gentleman, stern
Von Trapp Children (6)	scared of dad, mean to maria,
Maria accepting	sweet, beautiful, pure, soft headed
Nazis	evil mean

Gone With the Wind

Characters	Characteristics
Scarlett O'Hara	beautiful, independent, snobby
Ashley Wilkes	handsome, dependent
Melanie Wilkes	sweet, friendly, fragile but strong
Rhett Butler	no soft eye, smart, jolly

Practice role shifting by imitating the narrators' descriptions of the characters.

Answers on page 104.

PAIR PRACTICE

Think of five famous people and describe them to your partner as if you've forgotten their names. Follow the guidelines for describing people given in Unit 8, and use role shifting when describing personality, mannerisms, or things the person has said or done. Continue until your partner recognizes the person and spells the name.

COMPREHENSION

Winning Numbers

Try your luck. We'll give you not one chance, but *five* chances to win!

Watch the characters on screen as they announce the winning numbers (all numbers are between 50 and 100). Stop the tape and write the numbers below. After filling in all the numbers, check them with the Answer Key (page 182). Count how many numbers you read correctly, and write the number correct in the column on the right.

	Winning Numbers	Number Correct
Game 1.	66 53 98 69 86	4
Game 2.	88 76 59 87 64	5
Game 3.	55 68 58 78 73	3
Game 4.	77 67 78 91 97	5
Game 5.	99 98 52 96 68	5

Answer on page 104.

A Fishy Story

Ron tells a story about two good friends, Bob and Jack, who grew up in the same town. They both love to go fishing. Jack has great luck, while Bob never catches anything.

This narrative tells about Bob's many attempts to find the secret of Jack's success.

Summary given on page 105.

End of Unit 11

KEY PHRASES

Ask if opinion about teacher is true

Correct common misperception about teacher

Contrast qualities of parents

66

VOCABULARY REVIEW

opposites

PERSONAL QUALITIES

 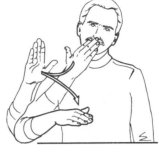

opposites

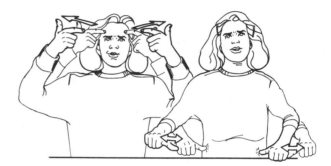

opposites

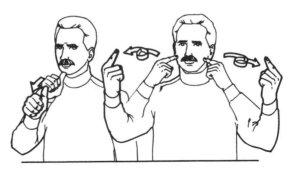

PERSONAL QUALITIES
ATTRIBUTED TO
CHARACTERS IN

*"Snow White and
the Seven Dwarfs"*

Snow White

Stepmother

Prince

Doc

Sleepy

Grumpy

Happy

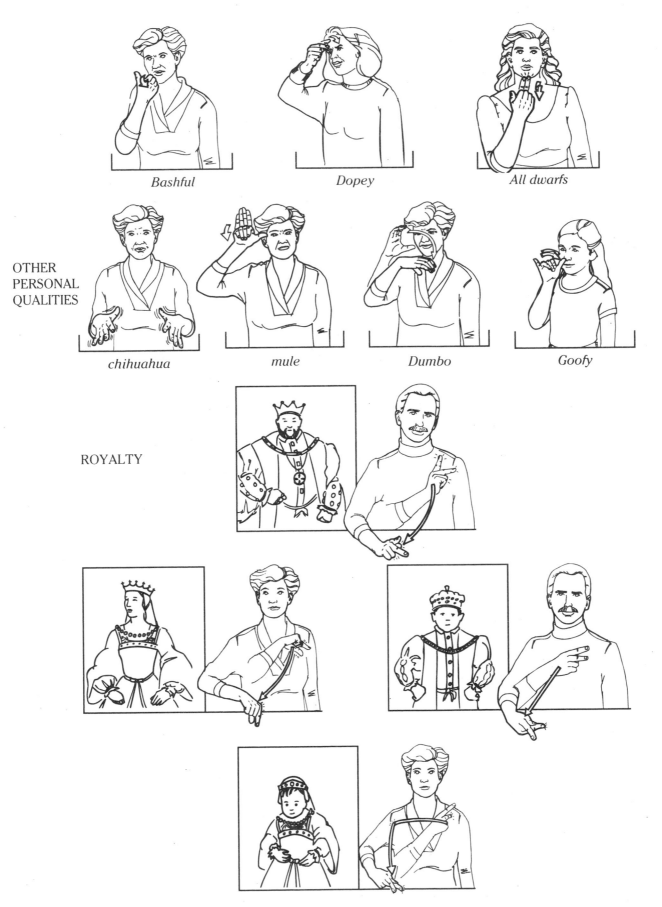

Bashful

Dopey

All dwarfs

OTHER
PERSONAL
QUALITIES

chihuahua

mule

Dumbo

Goofy

ROYALTY

PETS

NUMBERS
(twist to left)

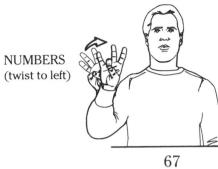

67

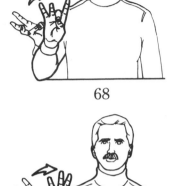

68

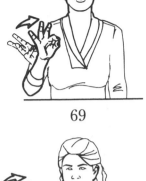

69

78

79

89

NUMBERS
(twist to right)

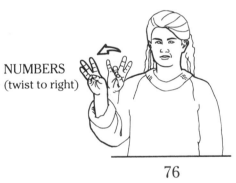

76

86

87

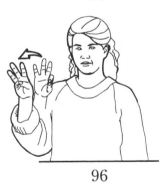

96

97

98

* If you are left-handed, movements are reversed.

Unit 12
Talking About Routines

LANGUAGE IN ACTION

Conversation

Mary (A) and her husband Ron (B) are at home. Mary is talking on the TTY with an Avon salesperson who wants to make an appointment to meet with them.

A: get husband's attention, **explain situation, ask when** salesperson can come
B: suggest Wednesday night
A: remind B of other plans for that night (PTA meeting)
B: suggest another night and time that week
A: describe routine, agree
B: respond
A: (return to TTY), **explain situation** with salesperson, ask if a later time that night would be OK
B: agree, but express condition (you go to bed at 11 p.m.)
A: (return to TTY) tell B that it is OK (end phone conversation)
B: (suddenly remember, wave to get attention)
A: (hang up phone, look at B)
B: tell A that her parents are coming to visit that night
A: respond, (dial phone again)

Key phrases that express target language functions are highlighted. Replay the videotape until you can follow the conversation without the aid of the cues. Then rehearse the conversation, especially the key phrases.

CONVERSATION PRACTICE

To practice the key phrases in a new context, find a partner and role play the situation below:

Situation: There has been a big change in your life. Discuss with your partner how this has changed your routine. (Possible changes: you got married, had a baby, got a new puppy, started a new job, broke your leg, your grandmother moved in.)

GRAMMAR NOTES
Clock Numbers

To tell the time from 1 to 12 o'clock, first sign "time" (index finger taps the wrist of the non-dominant hand), then sign the number indicating the hour.

For 1 - 9 o'clock, the number is signed with a slight waving movement in the fingerspelling area of the signing space. The numbers for 10, 11, and 12 o'clock are signed without the waving movement.

For 1 - 9 o'clock, the sign combination "time" + number is often contracted so that the number indicating the hour begins at the wrist of the non-dominant hand, and then moves to the fingerspelling area.

Hour and Minute Information. For combinations of hour and minute information, sign the number for the hour, then slightly to the right of that, sign the number for minutes. (Left-handed signers sign minutes slightly to the left.) There is no waving movement, and the sign for "time" does not usually precede the numbers. For the first nine minutes (:01 - :09), sign ZERO then the number, i.e.:

7:05 = SEVEN, ZERO FIVE.

Numbers 1 - 9 are signed with the palm facing away from the body for both hour and minute information; the rest of the numbers are signed just like the cardinal (or counting) numbers.

GRAMMAR PRACTICE

Clock Numbers

Ella will now model clock numbers on screen. Notice the direction her palm faces, the waving movement for numbers 1 - 9, and how she gives combined hour and minute information. Replay the tape and practice each number sign.

CALENDAR, PART 2

Cinnie will model four sentences saying when and how often an activity occurs. Two sentences indicate every week on the same day (i.e., "every Tuesday"). The other sentences indicate every day in the week, the same part of the day (i.e., "every evening next week"). See how the calendars below are marked to indicate the information given in each sentence.

For this activity, today is the *16th of the month.*

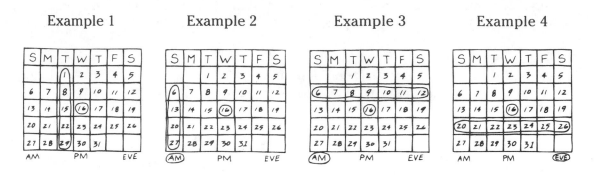

Example 1   Example 2   Example 3   Example 4

Activity. Brian will now sign four sentences saying when and how often activities occur. Mark the calendars to indicate the information given. Circle the part of the day if it is given.

1.   2.   3.   4.

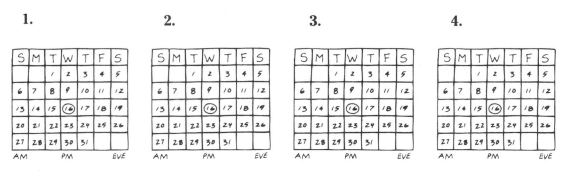

Answers on page 105.

Now rewind the tape and practice signing the sentences. Pay attention to the order in which the time information is given.

COMPREHENSION

What Time?

On screen several signers will tell you what they did at specific times. After each sentence, stop the tape and record the time, circle the part of the day, and write in the activity below.

Example:

time: __8:30__ (a.m.) activity: _____ get dressed _____ — clothes circle motions
          p.m.
          eve.

time: __945__ a.m. activity: __husband and i serious talk__
          p.m.
          (eve.)

time: __7:15__ (a.m.) activity: __made food then did eat__
          p.m.
          eve.

time: __615__ a.m. activity: __friend call__
          p.m.
          (eve.)

time: __10__ (a.m) activity: __go to french class__
          p.m.
          eve.

time: __1230__ (a.m.) activity: __goodbye then left__
          p.m.
          eve.

time: __3__ a.m. activity: __rooster crowing__
          (p.m.)
          eve.

time: __11:45__ a.m. activity: __get in bed__
          p.m.
          (eve.)

time: __4:30__ a.m. activity: __help children with hw__
          (p.m.)
          eve.

Answers on page 105.

Safe Keeping

Mary tells a story about a woman hiding money in a safe place, but then forgetting where she put it. She goes on to tell how the woman and her husband searched for the money.

How much money did the woman hide? _____

List all the places the couple looked for the money: _____

_____

_____

Where did they finally find the money? _____

Summary given on page 105.

CULTURE/LANGUAGE NOTES
Brief History of Deaf America

In 1817 Laurent Clerc, a Deaf teacher from the National Royal Institution for the Deaf in Paris, came to the United States to help Thomas H. Gallaudet, a hearing American, start America's first School for the Deaf in Hartford, Connecticut. Clerc brought from the Paris school a highly effective teaching method using Sign Language, the language of Deaf people.

Graduates of the Hartford School went on to establish similar residential Schools for the Deaf in other states. Many Deaf people became teachers of the Deaf and Sign Language was the language of instruction in the classroom. Then in 1864, the first university for the Deaf (now called Gallaudet University) was established by a charter signed by President Lincoln.

Late in the 19th century the tide began to turn against Deaf people and their language. In 1880, the International Congress on Education of the Deaf in Milan, Italy adopted a resolution banning the use of Sign Language in teaching deaf children. The "oral method" of teaching gained momentum; speech and lipreading became the primary educational goal. Deaf people were discouraged from entering the teaching profession, and Sign Language was no longer permitted in the classroom.

Also in 1880 the National Association of the Deaf (NAD) was founded in Cincinnati, Ohio. This organization brought Deaf people together from around the country to work for their common interests and fight discrimination in schools and workplaces. Around the turn of the century, because of a growing concern that American Sign Language would be lost, the NAD established a fund used to make a series of films in Sign Language. One of these films is George Veditz's *Preservation of Sign Language*. Over the years, the NAD has fought public ignorance of deafness, underemployment of Deaf people, discrimination against Deaf people who were denied driver's licenses, discrimination against Deaf teachers, double tax exemption for Deaf people, and the strictly oral method in education of the Deaf.

The years from 1900 to 1960 could be considered the "Dark Ages" of Deaf history. What sustained the community during this period of strong oralism and lack of social understanding was the Deaf clubs. Local clubs provided a place where Deaf people could congregate to socialize, share the latest news, organize around political issues, plan events and outings, and, in later years, watch captioned films. The clubs nourished the sense of group loyalty and community, maintained the culture, and preserved the cherished language.

In 1901 the National Fraternal Society of the Deaf (NFSD) was formed to provide insurance to Deaf people. Initially providing burial benefits to members, the "Frat" expanded to include life, sickness, and accident insurance, and later fought discrimination against Deaf drivers in getting automobile insurance.

Through the years of the First World War and the depression, attempts to improve Deaf people's lives were not given priority, as was true for most minority groups. During the 1940's, however, the NAD was successful in getting the Civil Service Commission to revoke a ruling that discriminated against Deaf printers, making lucrative positions available to many Deaf people. During World War II, many Deaf people became "soldiers on the assembly line,"* performing a large variety of jobs and demonstrating that the abilities of Deaf people can contribute to any work force.

The 1960's ushered in an era of change, as evidenced by the following milestones:

- Teletypewriters for the Deaf (TTYs) were invented by a deaf man in 1964 and began to take hold during the 1970's. Later, with the invention of telecaption decoders, television too became accessible to deaf people.

- The National Registry of Interpreters for the Deaf was founded in 1964, leading to increased respect for, and greater proficiency within, the profession.

- The first linguistic study of American Sign Language was published in 1965. The study was made by William Stokoe at Gallaudet and had great impact on continued research and recognition of ASL.

- The educational philosophy of "Total Communication" began to gain acceptance, and signs were again permitted in the schools.

- In 1966, the NAD fought for the right of a Deaf couple in California to adopt a foster child. The judge had said that the child would not have a normal home environment with Deaf parents. After an outpouring of support from the Deaf communities all over the U.S., the couple was awarded custody of the child.

- The National Theatre of the Deaf first toured in 1967, spreading awareness and appreciation of ASL throughout the world.

- Section 504 of the Rehabilitation Act of 1973 (often called the civil rights act for disabled people) was finally signed into law in 1976. This law requires that any institution receiving federal funds be accessible to all disabled people. Sign Language interpreting services began to be provided at many colleges around the country, as well as in hospitals, courtrooms, government agencies and various workplaces.

*Jack R. Gannon, *Deaf Heritage: A Narrative History of Deaf America*, National Association of the Deaf, Silver Spring, Maryland, 1981, p. 222. For more information on the history of Deaf America, see Gannon's book and other NAD publications, as well as Harlan Lane, *When The Mind Hears: A History of the Deaf*, Random House, NY, 1984.

- In 1979, when the movie Voices was produced featuring a hearing performer in the role of a Deaf character, Deaf people staged a successful boycott of the movie in several cities, forcing the distributor to withdraw the film from the market. Since then, Deaf performers have become more visible on television, stage, and film, and Deaf people are more often hired to perform in Deaf roles.

In recent years, there has been increased academic acceptance of American Sign Language in colleges and universities. There has also been a growing recognition of Deaf culture by the general public. Deaf individuals are beginning to attain decision-making positions where they can make a difference in the lives of Deaf people. The "Deaf President Now" rally at Gallaudet University in the spring of 1988 drew widespread support not only from members of the Deaf community, but from many people in all walks of life. What happened at Gallaudet that fateful week was the culmination of a people's struggle to break the chains of paternalism. This struggle for Deaf rights and self-determination continues. The protest at Gallaudet is seen by many as the beginning of a new chapter in the life of Deaf America.

End of Unit 12

KEY PHRASES

Ask what time person usually gets up

Tell what time you usually get up

Tell what you do every Tuesday

Tell what you do once a month

Tell about your morning routine

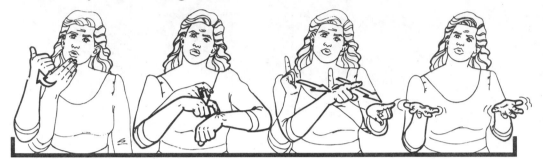

Ask what is a good time to go

VOCABULARY REVIEW

MORNING
ROUTINE

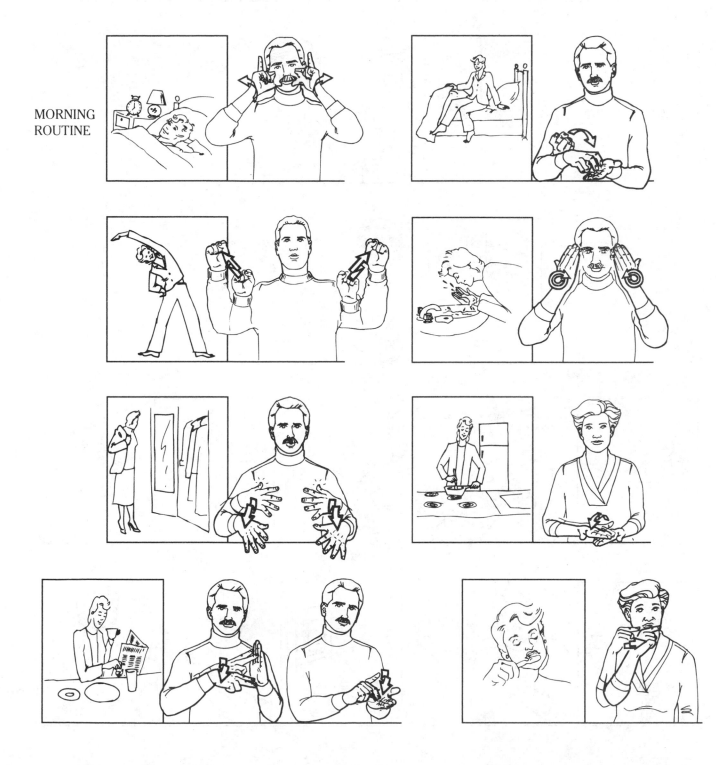

EVENING ROUTINE

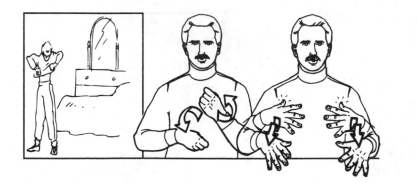

TIME SIGNS
Frequency

HOW OFTEN

always — never

LENGTH OF TIME

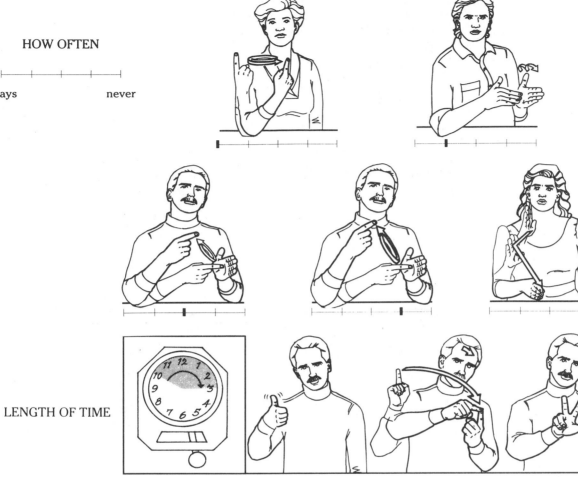

BEFORE/AFTER

APPROXIMATE TIME
(around 8:00)

WAYS TO WAKE UP

GETTING
READY

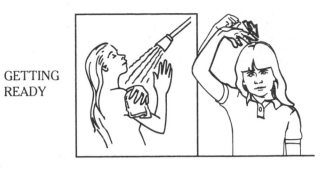

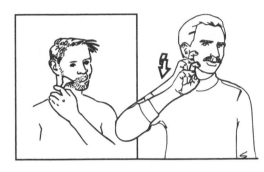

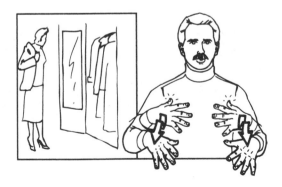

ROOMS IN THE HOUSE

WH-WORD
QUESTION SIGNS

CLOCK NUMBERS

1:00

2:00

3:00

4:00

5:00

6:00

7:00

8:00

9:00

10:00

11:00

12:00

MINUTE/HOUR

Units 7 – 12
Cumulative Review

LANGUAGE AND CULTURE

Interrupting Conversations

On screen you will see several situations which focus on acceptable ways to interrupt conversations. Observe the attention-getting behaviors and phrases used to begin the interruptions. (These scenes were filmed in an informal situation, among people who know each other. Interrupting behaviors would vary in other situations.)

After you view the situations, read the summary of culturally appropriate behaviors that follows.

SUMMARY NOTES

When you are in situations where you know the people involved, you can interrupt conversations the ways you saw on screen. Otherwise, you may want to wait until you are acknowledged before interrupting.

How do you know when it's an appropriate time to interrupt a conversation? Some situations are obvious - while interruptions are commonplace at parties or social events, we are expected not to interrupt private conversations. Unfortunately, most situations are less obvious. The interrupter needs to look for clues to decide when to interrupt. For example, consider where the signers are in relation to other people (i.e., standing with their backs to others), the seriousness of the conversation, and the urgency of your message.

How do you interrupt a conversation? The approach you use depends on the situation. If it is a casual conversation, you may walk right up and get the attention of the person you wish to speak to by waving or touching his/her shoulder. If the conversation looks intense or you're unsure of the appropriateness of the interruption, then stand and wait at a polite distance to indicate that you are waiting for a chance to talk.

Once the signer acknowledges you, apologize for the interruption and explain why you wanted the person's attention. The signer may acknowledge you but ask you to wait for a second; you should then wait for eye contact that indicates it's your turn.

Handling Auditory Interruptions. In Dialogue 4 of the classroom videotape, a Deaf man was talking with the hearing receptionist at a Deaf service agency when the phone rang. The receptionist handled the interruption by asking the man to wait, informing him that the phone was ringing, and asking the caller to hold. She was then able to resume the conversation.

It is important to develop your skill in handling auditory interruptions, as they may occur frequently while you interact with Deaf people. If you are involved in a conversation and break eye contact because you hear the phone ring or someone calls your name, you should **inform the Deaf person** why you looked away. Simply say, "just a sec, the telephone " or "excuse me, someone's knocking on the door," etc. This way the Deaf person knows why you looked away.

92

knocking on the door," etc. This way the Deaf person knows why you are distracted and can adjust to the information. Breaking eye contact without an explanation is considered rude; it looks like you are inattentive or not interested in the conversation.

Closing Conversations

On screen, you will see Mary and Ella modeling phrases to use in ending conversations. Practice these phrases.

PAIR PRACTICE

Practice the behaviors you saw on screen by role playing the following situations with two other people:

Situation 1: At a party, the host is explaining something to someone. You need to ask the host if s/he has more 7-Up (or where you can find a bottle opener).

Situation 2: A friend is giving you instructions on how to get to the nearest ice cream store. Your 10-year-old son taps you excitedly in order to show you something he has found in the backyard. You tell him to wait until your friend finishes talking.

Situation 3: You're talking with your friend Jane on the phone. It so happens that Jane knows Willie, the Deaf person you work with, and wishes him to contact her.

Willie is talking with another person in the far corner of the room. Interrupt them to explain the situation and to ask for Willie's phone number so you can give it to Jane.

Situation 4: Two Deaf friends are having a serious discussion in the far corner of the room near a door. Inform them that someone is knocking at the door.

Situation 5: Ask the person sitting in the middle of the couch to get Judy's attention. (Judy is sitting next to the person, reading the newspaper.) Then ask Judy what time a certain movie is playing.

Situation 6: You and a Deaf woman are standing in the middle of the sidewalk in a park. The woman is telling you about her weekend when you see a person on rollerskates approaching. The Deaf woman is not aware that the skater is about to pass her. Interrupt to caution her.

Situation 7: You're having a great conversation with a person at a party, but you need to go home because the babysitter is expecting you. Explain to your friend that you have to leave now.

Situation 8: You've been talking with a friend for quite a while, and you need to make a phone call. Excuse yourself but tell your friend you'll be right back.

Situation 9: You're just finishing a conversation, but before you go, check with your friend to confirm the dinner appointment for next Wednesday night.

GRAMMAR PRACTICE

Analyzing Numbers

On screen, several signers will sign sentences incorporating a number sign. After each sentence, write down the number and circle the number type.

Number		*Number Type*			
1._____	cardinal	cents	age	clock	ordinal
2._____	cardinal	cents	age	clock	ordinal
3._____	cardinal	cents	age	clock	ordinal
4._____	cardinal	cents	age	clock	ordinal
5._____	cardinal	cents	age	clock	ordinal
6._____	cardinal	cents	age	clock	ordinal
7._____	cardinal	cents	age	clock	ordinal
8._____	cardinal	cents	age	clock	ordinal
9._____	cardinal	cents	age	clock	ordinal
10._____	cardinal	cents	age	clock	ordinal
11._____	cardinal	cents	age	clock	ordinal
12._____	cardinal	cents	age	clock	ordinal
13._____	cardinal	cents	age	clock	ordinal
14._____	cardinal	cents	age	clock	ordinal
15._____	cardinal	cents	age	clock	ordinal

Answers on page 105.

Questions to Ask

Now that you are at the end of Level 1, you should be able to ask the following questions. Read the cue for each question, think about how you would ask it, and watch Cinnie model the question on screen. Then find a partner and practice signing the questions (and answers) to each other.

1. ask if the other person has already eaten

2. offer to bring the other person something to drink

3. ask the other person if she wants to go out to eat with you

4. ask the other person where s/he works

5. ask the other person to describe what s/he does at work

6. ask the other person how old his/her father is

7. ask the other person what time the two of you will meet at the movie theatre next Tuesday

8. ask the other person what color Ian's new car is

9. ask the other person how many brother and sisters s/he has

10. ask the other person where s/he ranks among siblings

11. ask if what you heard about a physician is true

12. ask the other person how long his/her parents have been married

13. ask the other person how long s/he has been working as a carpenter

14. ask the other person what s/he and his/her friend will be doing at a specific time on a specific day

15. ask the other person when his/her daughter's birthday is

16. ask the other person if an item in the room belongs to him/her

17. ask how the other person is getting to a party next Saturday night

18. ask if directions to a particular location are correct

19. ask the other person how s/he gets along with his/her boss

20. identify and describe someone in the room, then ask the other person who s/he is

CULTURE/LANGUAGE NOTES

Maintaining Continuity in Relationships

One day, a Deaf woman was invited to a beginning ASL class. The instructor introduced the woman by giving information about her community ties and her personal life. Then students were asked to introduce themselves, and include information such as marital status, number of children, line of work, and any other personal comments. The visitor chatted briefly about these things with each student. (There were about twenty students in the class.) After the last student introduced herself, she jokingly said to the visitor, "That's a lot to remember." The visitor replied, "I remember most of it," and proceeded to amaze the class by going around the room restating information about each student, pointing out similarities between students' lives, and recalling personal comments.

The students thought the visitor had an exceptional memory. The instructor explained, however, that she possessed no extraordinary talent, but rather reflected a learned cultural behavior. She had done what most Deaf persons do naturally she attended to information that establishes a person's community ties, that assists her in identifying that person to others in the community, and that helps her maintain continuity in the relationship (or in this case the "acquaintanceship").

Deaf culture is called a "high-context" culture. Deaf people have an extensive information-sharing network among families, friends, and community members, and are involved in a host of familiar relationships. Among Deaf people, there is a great deal of shared knowledge, common experiences, goals and beliefs, common friends and acquaintances, a common way of talking; that is, their lives share a common context.

When two Deaf people meet for the first time, they establish this context by giving information about their community ties. They attend to specific information and retain it. When they meet again, they expect each other to remember their previous exchange and will begin to talk from that basis. Each will learn a little more about the other, which in turn will be remembered. This maintains continuity not only in that relationship; the information is fed back into the information-sharing network to help contextualize each person in relationship to the overall fabric of the community.

As you begin to meet Deaf people in and out of the classroom, you should volunteer information about yourself and make a point of retaining relevant information about others. The next time you meet, you should be able to recall the information exchanged in the first meeting, and from that context begin to build a relationship. Your ability to maintain continuity in relationships depends on your ability to remember relevant information about people. This developed skill will allow you to understand and participate in conversational patterns common in the Deaf community.

End of Cumulative Review: Units 7–12

KEY PHRASES

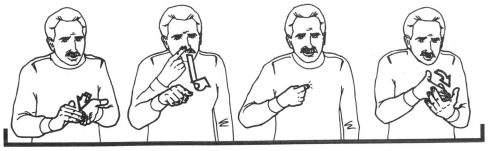

Interrupting conversation

Interrupting conversation to relay a message

Ending a conversation (phrase 1)

Ending a conversation (phrase 2)

Ending a conversation (phrase 3)

Ask to hold conversation

Ask how much it costs

VOCABULARY REVIEW

WAYS TO ASK FOR
CLARIFICATION

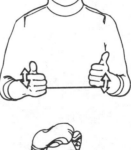

WAYS TO GIVE
FEEDBACK AND
COMMENTS

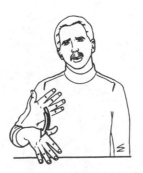

ANSWER KEY

UNIT 7

Fingerspelling, Part 3

1. ice
2. TV
3. diet
4. Coke
5. oil
6. fun
7. HS
8. apt
9. 7-Up
10. TTY
11. van
12. cake

The Candy Bar

A man went to the airport and stood in line to buy his ticket. When he got to the ticket counter he found out that his flight had been delayed. He decided to buy a newspaper, a candy bar and a cup of coffee. He found a seat, made himself comfortable and started reading the newspaper. He soon noticed the man sitting next to him take a bite of the candy bar. He was astonished, gave him a dirty look and then took a bite of the candy bar himself. The other man had the same reaction and popped the rest of the candy into his mouth. The first man was really furious, but just then, he heard it was time to board the plane. He got on the plane and sat down. After the plane took off, he reached into his back pocket to get a comb, and instead pulled out the candy bar that he had bought.

UNIT 8

Personal Data

deaf

used to be married,
now divorced

Jamie

likes to go to
the movies

Sean

has six
children

Missing Number

1. 40
2. 44
3. 60
4. 25
5. 70

UNIT 9
Give and Take

Who?	How Much?
1. Sally	none
2. Jane	35 cents
3. Bob	none
4. Bob	30 cents
5. Sally	30 cents

Making Requests

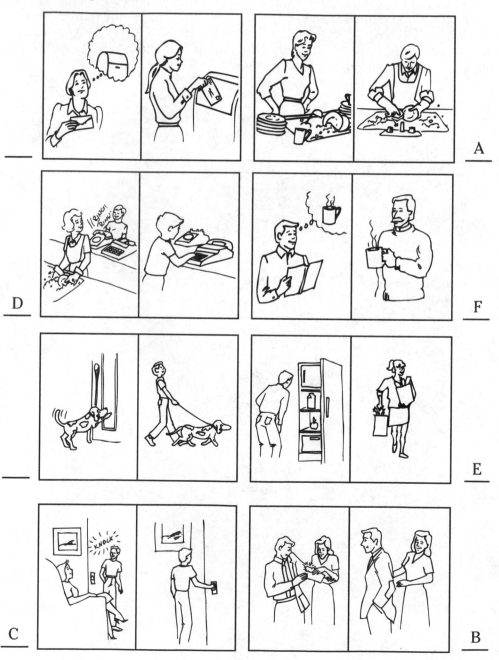

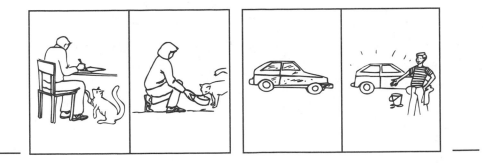

ABC Gum

After the boy stuck the gum on the bench and went home, a man sat on the bench to read a book. When he was ready to get up, he found the gum sticking to his pants. In disgust, he removed it and threw it on the sidewalk. A woman walked by and stepped on it. She removed it from her shoe and flung it at a tree where it stuck. Later, two young lovers came along and stopped under the tree. The girl leaned against the tree and the boy rested his hand against the trunk as he talked to her. Upon leaving, he pulled his hand away only to find it stuck to the gum. He pitched the gum onto the bench. Finally, the boy returned to find the gum in the same place. He popped it into his mouth and started blowing bubbles.

UNIT 10

Talking About Children

eldest: 36-year-old son — married, works as a printer
second: 33-year-old son — divorced, teaches at a state School for the Deaf
third: 31-year-old daughter — married, works with computers
fourth: 27-year-old daughter — single, works at a bank
fifth: 27-year-old son — separated, looking for a job
sixth: 24-year-old daughter — now attending college, has a steady boyfriend

A Show of Hands

1. Contestant 1 (standing closest to the game show host)
     her name is Carol
     her family is not present because they live far away
     she is not married
     she has two younger brothers
     she is a manager at a factory
  Contestant 2
     her name is Janie
     she is married
     she has four children:
       oldest is seven years old(girl),
       second oldest is six years old(girl),
       third is a four-year-old boy,
       the youngest is a three-year-old boy.
     she works as a lab technician at a hospital nearby

2. Name three Deaf publishers.
3. DawnSignPress, NAD, and Silent News
4. Name three well-known Deaf female artists
5. Betty Miller, Regina O. Hughes, and Linda Bove
6. Linda Bove, because she is an actress, not an artist
7. Linda Tom

Fingerspelling, Part 4

1. Wl
2. EE
3. NT
4. OY
5. NN
6. ING
7. GL
8. GHT

UNIT 11

Describing Characters

The Ten Commandments

Characters

Pharaoh	cruel, arrogant, wealthy
Jewish slaves	fearful, complaining
Moses	good, humble, wise and courageous

The Sound of Music

Characters — *Characteristics*

Baron Von Trapp	good-looking, gentlemanly, stern
Von Trapp children	frightened (of Dad), rude (to Maria), mischievous
Maria	sweet, pretty, innocent, accepting, soft-hearted
The Nazis (soldiers)	evil, mean

Gone With the Wind

Characters — *Characteristics*

Scarlett O'Hara	beautiful, strong, independent, snobbish
Ashley Wilkes	handsome, cowardly, dependent on others
Melanie Wilkes	sweet, friendly, fragile but strong, homely handsome,
Rhett Butler	arrogant, boastful, bright, independent, gentlemanly

Winning Numbers

Game 1. 66, 53, 98, 79, 86
Game 2. 88, 76, 59, 87, 64
Game 3. 55, 83, 58, 69, 73
Game 4. 77, 67, 98, 91, 97
Game 5. 99, 78, 52, 96, 68

A Fishy Story

To figure out the secret of Jack's success, the first thing Bob did was to buy exactly the same kind of fishing pole that Jack used. To assure success he asked Jack if he could switch fishing spots with him. Bob then thought it might be Jack's clothes that did the trick. One day when Jack was away, Bob snuck into Jack's house, took his fishing outfit and his fishing pole, and even his worms. Bob then went to one of Jack's fishing spots, and started to fish. A fish came up out of the water and remarked "Hey, you're not Jackwhere's Jack?" Bob was so stunned he dropped the pole.

UNIT 12

Calendar, Part 2

1. Every Wednesday (2,9,16,23,30)
2. Every afternoon this week (14,15,16,17,18)
3. Each day at 12:00 noon next week (21,22,23,24,25)
4. Every Monday night (7,14,21,28)

What Time?

1. 9:45 eve, husband and I had a serious discussion
2. 7:15 a.m., made breakfast, then fed the cat
3. 6:15 eve, friend rings me up
4. 10:00 a.m., you go to your French class
5. 12:30 a.m., said goodbye, then left
6. 3:00 p.m., rooster crowing
7. 11:45 eve, get in bed
8. 4:30 p.m., help children with their homework

Safe Keeping

A married couple had been planning to go on vacation. The week before the trip, the husband asked his wife to withdraw a hundred dollars from the bank. After withdrawing the money, the woman decided to hide it in a safe place. As the vacation neared, the husband asked about the money, but she could not remember where she hid it. The two of them searched everywhere (under chair cushion, in every book on the shelves, under the lamp, on top of the dishes and inside the cups in the kitchen cabinets, under the mattress, inside the dresser drawers, and inside the pockets of the coat in the closet. Finally, the woman found the money behind a picture on the wall. Her husband told her he thought it was a lousy place to hide the money, and she retorted, "Lousy? Hmmph."

CUMULATIVE REVIEW: UNITS 7-12

Analyzing Numbers

1.	67	cardinal	9.	8	ordinal
2.	5	cents	10.	10:45	clock
3.	47	age	11.	75	cents
4.	9:15	clock	12.	2:30	clock
5.	2	ordinal	13.	43	cardinal
6.	6	ordinal	14.	28	cents
7.	29	age	15.	15	age
8.	60	cardinal			

End of Answer Key